# Journey to a new universe

C. R. Noval

BookLeaf
Publishing

India | USA | UK

Presentation by *BookLeaf Publishing*

Web: www.bookleafpub.com

E-mail: info@bookleafpub.com

ISBN: 9789357212199

First edition 2023

# DEDICATION

For my grandmother, who taught me the love of reading,

To my mom and dad, who taught me the love of science and life,

and for my husband, who taught me the love of dreaming.

# PREFACE

All those who dream of writing a book must already know there is no perfect time for it. Therefore, this book was not born at the perfect time. This book emerged in a chaotic and imperfect moment, full of dreadful deadlines, sleepless nights, days of research, and afternoons of frantic writing. But like every book, it was also born from the desire to write my deepest feelings, hoping that they reach someone. I hope that someone is you.

# Our Journey

Embrace your journey since you are the only
traveler.
Start at dawn, at noon, at midnight, no matter
what.
You won't be late for your own travel.
Raise the anchors and hoist the sails
Of your own free will, and prepare your
astrolabe.
You may need it when life unravels.
Do not get carried away by the haste
Of those who sail with their own ships.
Let yourself be accompanied by whales.
Follow the rhythm of your breeze.
Draw your map with invisible lines,
Choose your breaks and your ports,
And run rampant through the ocean's sun.
Fly over the waves, defeat your monsters
Create your mermaids, and follow the thunder.
Paint your cruise ship with your banners.
Enjoy your voyage! There is only one,
And that's all that matters.

# Expectations

She could be the wind and the storm that rages over the sea,
But she decided instead to be the morning breeze.
She could have been lightning and thunder echoing in the dark,
But she was the rays of light that enter your window at dawn.
She could have been tornadoes, tsunamis, and typhoons,
But she preferred to be the clouds that float calmly above the world.

Everyone expects her to be mountains, oceans, and deserts:
To split the world in two like an impressive earthquake,
But she wanted to be the forest that covered gentle slopes,
Travel countries like a river full of meanders and curves.
To be a hidden meadow full of simple wildflowers,
And become a peaceful night full of secrets and powers.

Everyone wanted her to be so many things,
And the only thing she wanted was to have a
pair of wings.
Everyone expected so much of her that she
couldn't help,
But wonder if her dreams were even hers.

# Books and pages

Pages and pages,
I read them, they nurtured me.
Hundreds of letters paraded through my eyes.
I bookmarked so many;
Some scared me, others moved me.

Book after book:
Most old and some new.
I cherish them, they shelter me.
And in the haze of my certainty,
I've kept most of them with me.

Words and sentences
Most of the time,
I hesitate about whether to write them or not.
But in the midst of my weariness, I forget them;
I am uncertain of their value or their worth.

Phrases and prose
That I covet like those roses
That I press against the sheets.
And I write them in my journal
With all those old treasured quotes.
I'll record them in my memory
to repeat them while I sleep.

Novels and titles,
I collect them as prizes that I can show the
world.
All their covers, I'll compile them.
I will keep them; they will nest me
As it has happened before.

# Old City, my Town…

Old city of mine, how shattered you are,
With your glow dimmed and your shine lost.
Old city of sand that crumbles and falls,
With your crooked streets of lost paths.
Old city so proud, with your worn cobblestones
And stone palaces that are falling apart.
With crowded houses that crack under the sun.


My city, so sad, slowly disappearing into the
ground.
Dipped into so much history and blood,
Your light fades as the buildings collapse.
My city is so small, with its hidden alleys
And a lonely tree to wish for better times.
With hundreds of columns and doves that flutter
around.
With its old squares and the children running
While their mothers pray, and their grandparents
wait
For the city to close at nine.


Where is my dear city now?
Old town found between dust and ruins.

Between fallen balconies and an endless wall
that I no longer want to walk.
Where is the laughter and the "Son"?
Where are the flashy dresses and the music out
loud?

Old city, my town!
When I go back, will you still be the same?
Or have you changed so much that I'll never be
able to see you again
Except in my mind?

Author note: "Son" is a genre of Cuban music.

# Little things

Those little things that make me,
They create me; they undo me.
Those little things that I long for,
That dismantle me, that destroy me.

These little things that I yearn for,
That I wish I could just tell you.
Those small trinkets that you gave me,
I collect them; I revere them.

I am a swarm of bees and gifts,
Of those small and pretty things:
Goodnight kisses, farewells,
Unused postcards, wistful smells.

I don't mind if you prefer
Those grand gestures that are a true display.
But big things don't make me live,
They don't make me smile at night.

I am all those little things,
A collection of my wings.
And with them, I could just fly,
Going far in the starry sky.

All those things that just complete me,
Make me human, make me simple.
All I want now is to show you
That those things just make me love you.

# Dark nights

While I'm sitting in the dark,
I can't help but see my past.
And I fail to grasp the wonders
That I am leaving far behind.
When I am thinking at night,
I can't help wasting my time.
And I lose not just the present,
But new memories to have.

How many hours did I spend
Dwelling on silly mistakes?
Unspoken words and broken smiles,
Sad heartaches that make me cry.
How many days did I waste
Rewinding songs that I just hate?
The ones I heard when I was low,
The ones I cried when he was gone.

And every time I look back,
I lose a part of my life.
I fill my senses with dark thoughts
That keep me from going far.
So, from this day on,
I will mess around no more.
I'll seize the moment, I'll see the light,
I'll seek my future, I'll build my life.

# Repeat this after a bad day

Take off your shoes,
Touch the grass, the sand, and the ground.
Breathe in, breathe out.
Fill your lungs with sound.

Relax your shoulders,
Calm down. You'll be fine.
Open your arms,
And lift your face towards the sky.

Close your eyelids,
Think of nothing.
Feel the wind flapping in the branches,
Empty your mind and smile.

Take off your shoes,
And you'll be fine.
The future is not here yet.
So, feel your skin, your hair, your hands.

Breathe in, breathe out.
There's no point in worrying now.
Life goes on, just like that.
Reach inside,
Everything will be alright.

# Rio

The waves caress the warm sand,
While the sun shines on the city.

The waves wash the white sand,
And the stairs are filled with people.

The waves touch the hot sand,
A thousand steps going up and down.

The sun tickles the bright sand,
And its light shines on the guns.

The waves break slowly on the land,
While the children smile and run.

The waves dance blue and warm.
All looking happy, fun and calm.

The sea crashes against the sand,
Keep your pockets closed and tight.

The waves wet the dry sand,
And stray bullets fly around.

The waves play around the land,
The favela is full of life.

The waves caress the warm sand,
While everyone tries to survive.

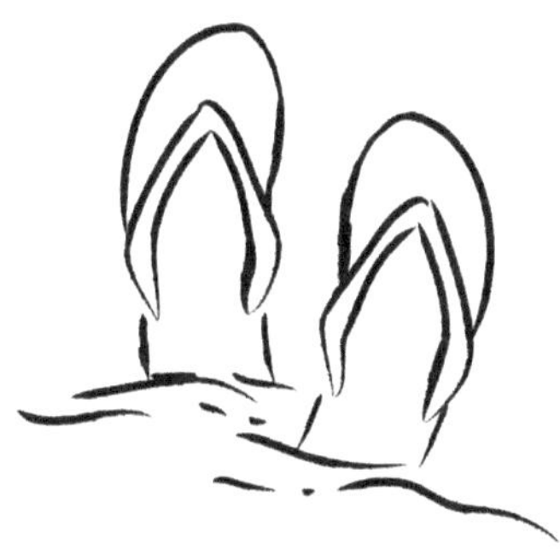

# Poem for Wandering Souls

It's a long way from here to my home.
To be honest, it's thousands of miles.
Different stars cover my eyes from the sky.
I wonder what they'll show me now.
Other humid winds mess up my hair,
And my feet wander through other salty lands.
Different constellations light up my night.
It's a long way from here to my home,
And I don't know when I can come back.

I'm alone now in the falling dark:
Wandering soul that cannot cry.
Other people talk to me, they are kind.
Their words mingle with their accents that I
can't understand.
I'm alone now, but I have to fight
To go through another day far from home, from
my house.
My heart aches with all the sorrows, but I cannot
stop right now.
It's a lonely road that I choose to explore.
It is an errant way for those who travel abroad.
I am away from home, and I want to go back,
But it's too late now.

# Dreaming

Every night when I go to sleep,
I fight with my brain,
I battle in my dreams.

Weaving cobwebs in my head,
Messing with the things I've read,
Rewriting echoes of my past,
Moving castles in my mind.

They become a kind of memory:
Cloudy facts, and hidden treasures.
And sometimes, I struggle in life
To decipher truth from lies.

Do I know you from a dream
Or a nightmare that I fear?
Did I travel far beyond?
Or did I never leave my home?

As the years pass, it's hard to say
What is true, and what is false.
And my mind just lags behind
What happens in real life.

But no matter what they say,
I prefer my dreams to stay.
I would rather live inside
Of the stories in my mind.

So, every night when I go to sleep,
I'm still fighting with my brain.
I win battles in my dreams.

# A single word

She wasn't a poem or a song
Or any of those cliché words.
She was sentences, paragraphs,
An illustrated book with photographs.
Chapters full of wandering words,
Pages with torn edges, crumbling margins,
All covered with hidden tarot cards.

She was not poetry, nor a ballad,
Not a cheesy phrase from that lullaby.
She was just fingers that flipped through pages,
Hands that bookmarked her corners,
And thoughts that created her cages.
She was a reader without a writer.
With broken pages like old scrolls,
Like an ancient tome eaten by moths,
Now coming off the tether, and losing her glow.

She contains a short story,
A novel, an encyclopedia,
A dedication without an epilogue,
A romantic novel with no happy ending.
A thousand letters in faded ink,
Old roses with bleached pink.
She contained so much.

But from time to time,
She wanted to contain nothing more.
Just lie down on the shore,
Empty her mind, and be a single word.

# Missing you, X

I miss you; I dream of you.
Every week or two.
All my dreams are blue
When I think of you.

I miss you; I think of you.
Some days more, some days less.
But sometimes, I go through life,
Carefree, happy, and nonchalant.
And sadness tinges my cheer
When I see that you are not here.

I miss you; I hear you.
When I close my eyes to sleep,
Your face wanders in my dreams.
And the months and time go by
Without seeing you on my nights.
But I wonder what you'll say
As your face slowly fades.

I miss sitting next to you,
Reading magic in a book.
Minutes, hours, and days passed
In our world made of glass.
But your smile was just enough
To convey a thousand words.

And I thought we had more time.
That the world would stop afterward.
But no matter how many months passed,
My heart keeps falling apart.
And the days keep turning smoothly,
And the leaves keep falling freely.
But I'll always think of you
Whenever I am dreaming.

# Snowfalls

When the snow falls
And the wind blows,
All the lights dim,
All the world sleeps.
And we sang songs
When it grew cold,
While the river is quiet,
And the hills are whiter.

When the snow falls,
There's nowhere to go,
The animals retreat,
Snowstorms close the streets.
And the sky is gray
As the sunlight fades,
While the wolves howl
Waking up the quiet owls.

And the forest is theirs
While winter covers their lairs.
And the stars shine
As the pine leaves dance.
And while nature calls,
And bears brawl,
All the warmth is gone,
Just when the snow falls.

# The things I want

I'd like to do the things that I want and not those
that I have to do.
I'd love to sleep all morning until the sun warms
my skin
And burns my eyelids, just because I can.
No hurrying or rushing…
Just morning being morning, slow, sleepy and
cozy.
No six am alarms, no cold breakfast at dawn.

Going through my days without haste, slowly
breathing the air.
My sun shines in the sky, gently caressing my
arms,
And waiting for me in bed, all the books I've
read.
A cup of coffee would accompany me from
afternoon to evening,
And all the way around, hot chocolate at dusk.
Eating breakfast for dinner, I would be such a
sinner.
Who would care about calories, swimsuits, or
Instagram galleries?
If food warms our souls, it should be more than
enough.

So, why instead of loving, caring for, and
hugging each other,
Are we caught in such a web?
Sleepless nights and dreamless days,
Gray mornings and blank pages,
And tiresome afternoons for miserable wages.
Let's hold each other more, hug us tightly,
Kiss our cheeks, and say good night.
Let's love each other more,
Say sweet dreams, trust ourselves, and keep us
close.

# For A

You took me by the hand and embraced my soul,
Without knowing me, slowly tempting me.
With your fingers in my hands, walking gently
by the sea,
With your arms around my back.
You hugged me senseless and opened a way
Towards tomorrow, until another day, towards
what will come next.
You sat with me without making a sound
Listening to me while I said more than a
thousand words.
Without judgment, with understanding,
Without hugging me, but without leaving me.
You walked by my side and made me smile
Without wanting it, and without trying.
Just because you already knew what I liked.
You complete me in ways I didn't know were
missing,
Just existing, breathing me gently.
Holding me tight, reading me softly.

# Save a bit of yourself

Save a bit of yourself for later, for dessert.
Leave some secrets concealed,
Like some crumbs hidden on your bedroom
floor.
Don't show all your mysteries,
The puzzles, and the riddles that wake you at
dawn.
Don't give all of yourself without fear or without
help.
Keep your essence untouchable.
Don't let others make you feel less.

I learned the hard way
That some days I feel bright
While on others days, I feel grey.
And in those moments I need
To take refuge in myself
As protection from the rain.

Save a little of your soul,
When you feel glum, when you feel cold.
Because with time, you realize
That if you give everything to the outside,
You are left with nothing behind.

# Fleeting Autumn

Everything falls; everything fades.
The smell of pumpkins fills the air.
The green has gone, and the fairies have come.
Withered leaves are blown by the wind,
Scattered on the sidewalks, running away,
Blocking roads, and filling in eaves.
The autumn breeze creates a flow of mustard
tones,
Reddish grass, brown fields, and wet stones.


Summer is gone, and everything falls around.
The world changes, the rain comes,
The sun hides behind the clouds
And squirrels hide their nuts.
Everything changes; the warmth is lost,
But the forest is full of life.
Maple leaves leave their mark,
On the dirty street, on the muddy road.
Death and decay surround us all.
But no matter where you look,
For a couple of weeks, for a couple of months,
Colorful trees still paint the hills.
Autumn is here, even just for a blink.

# Dreamless Nights

She sleeps and dreams of travel and books
With dragons to ride and princes to fight,
With mermaids and fairies and all kinds of
magic
That light up her mornings and keep her alive.

He sleeps and dreams of horses and wolves,
Of space ships and warriors heading to the West.
He thinks about glory, creating a story
Of conquest and fame while turning in bed.

They sleep, and when dreaming, they visit each
other.
They fight in their nightmares, they stroll on the
moon.
And on cold nights, she is holding his hands,
And warms him completely as if she were the
sun.

They dream and fear waking up at once
And not meeting again under cloudy skies.
They sleep and fear not seeing each other
anymore,
waking up in the morning without dreams and
without love.

# Imagine yourself

Look at you doing well and fine.
Forget all those treacherous doubts
That crawl under your skin.
Starting over is not easy or fair.
Don't listen to those voices of uncertainty:
Those who stop you,
Or those who coax you.
Always keep your head up in the air.


Break a couple of mirrors;
You don't need them to tell you that you are
beautiful.
Take a few detours through the park;
Your job is important but so is having peace of
mind.
Change your hairstyle, break your diet,
And close your ears to all those lies.
Follow some suggestions, any but mine.


Some days are tricky, but you will see
That you will last until the next night.
Close your ears to those old pieces of advice.
They will have years,

But these are your choices.
Dress for tomorrow, if not for today,
To keep your insecurity at bay.
Look at yourself, doing fine and well.

# Those Who Shaped Me

I've been shaped by those around me,
With whom I have talked for minutes
Or those with whom I have shared lives.
I've been cut to pieces and reimagined
By those who gave me air and those who gave
me life.
We danced in the street and walked together,
Talking about nonsense or about the weather,
Making me feel better just by holding my hand.
I feel so blessed to have so many shoulders
surrounding me:
Arms that helped me, and voices that armed me.
Friends who came and went so fast,
And dozens of others who stayed by my side.
I cried for some who left and played with
bubbles in my head.
Some people brought me light, others brought
me night,
Some walked with me for a couple of seconds,
While others ran for miles.
A few of them made me sing, but most made me
laugh.
Many of them stayed close, others waved at me
from afar.

I will be shaped by those around me until the
day I die.

# The Girl with the Gryffindor Scarf

Girl with the Gryffindor scarf.
Why are you so far?
In your little cafes with their hidden tables?
In those lengthy books with thousands of pages?

Girl that dreams so high…
What are you doing right now?
Wasting yourself on a long-term achievement?
Passing the days marking checkboxes?

Girl, why are you so shy?
Don't be so quiet; sing out loud.
Stop planning ahead, filling in pros and cons.
You don't have to be straight A's and gold.

Girl who wants to do it all;
Fulfilling tasks that are not even yours.
With your own wishes fading into the distance.
Do you really have time for all those
commitments?

Girl, why are you so sad?
Leaving your dreams behind.
Would you put yourself first for once?
Making decisions on your own.

Girl, you still have time to start turning things around.
Follow your steps, and you'll be fine.
Girl, don't be afraid to fight your mind.
Open your wings to the sky, and fly high.